Modern Parenting in a Tech-Driven Era

Franklin Fisher

Copyright © (2024) by Franklin Fisher

Published by Amazon KDP

Amazon.com, Inc.

P.O. Box 81226

Seattle, WA 98108-1226

United States.

Cover design by Amazon KDP

Printed by Amazon KDP in the USA

Table of Contents

Chapter 1

Introduction to Contemporary Parenting

Exploring the Evolution of Parenting Approaches

Parenting is a fluid concept, adapting over time to cater to the changing needs of children within diverse historical and cultural contexts. To grasp the essence of modern parenting, it's imperative to trace the evolution of parenting styles through the ages.

Traditional Parenting

Emphasis on Authority and Firm Discipline Historically, parenting leaned heavily on authoritarian models characterized by strict discipline, obedience, and control. Parents were viewed as paramount authority figures, tasked with enforcing rules and upholding societal norms. This approach, prevalent across many cultures, often relied on punitive measures to correct behavior.

The Transition to Permissive Parenting

In the mid-20th century, there was a noticeable shift towards permissive parenting styles, influenced notably by psychologists such as Dr. Benjamin Spock. This method advocated for greater leniency, nurturing, and responsiveness to children's needs. Permissive parents tended to grant children more autonomy to explore and express themselves, prioritizing emotional support over rigid discipline.

The Emergence of Authoritative Parenting

In the late 20th century, authoritative parenting gained traction as a balanced approach. This style amalgamates high responsiveness with high expectations. Authoritative parents establish clear guidelines and expectations while remaining supportive and communicative. They foster independence while upholding consistent boundaries, aiming to raise self-disciplined and socially adept children.

Helicopter and Free-Range

Parenting In recent years, parenting styles have diversified further. Helicopter parenting, describing overly involved parents who micromanage their children's lives, contrasts with free-range parenting, which advocates for granting children more independence and freedom to explore with minimal oversight.

The Era of Tech-Savvy Parenting

Today, the integration of technology into daily life has ushered in the era of tech-savvy parenting. This contemporary approach necessitates navigating a digital landscape and balancing the advantages and risks of technology. Tech-savvy parents must be well-versed in digital tools, social media, and online safety while promoting healthy screen habits.

The Influence of Technology on Family Dynamics

The rapid advancement of technology has profoundly reshaped family dynamics, altering how parents and children interact, communicate, and relate to one another.

Shifts in Communication Patterns

One of the most notable impacts of technology on family dynamics is the transformation of communication patterns. Smartphones, tablets, and computers enable families to stay connected regardless of distance. While instant messaging, video calls, and social media facilitate real-time communication, they also present challenges such as decreased face-to-face interactions and fragmented attention during family time.

Balancing work and family life

Technology blurs the boundaries between work and family life. Remote work and flexible job arrangements allow parents to be more present at home, enhancing family bonding. However, this flexibility can lead to work encroaching on family time, necessitating a delicate balance between professional commitments and family life.

Educational opportunities and challenges

The integration of technology in education offers new avenues for learning and development. Educational apps, online courses, and interactive platforms provide children with access to diverse resources.

Yet, excessive screen time poses health concerns, necessitating parental monitoring and regulation.

Social development and peer relationships

Social media and online gaming platforms redefine how children form and maintain peer relationships. While these digital spaces foster social interaction and community building, they also expose children to risks such as cyberbullying and inappropriate content, highlighting the importance of parental guidance and education on online safety.

Parental Roles and Responsibilities in the Digital Age

Technology redefines parental roles and responsibilities, requiring parents to be digital role models and educators. Open communication about technology is crucial for guiding children through the complexities of the digital world, fostering trust, and creating a supportive environment.

Chapter 2

Grasping the Digital Terrain

In today's swiftly evolving technological realm, digital gadgets and platforms wield immense influence over the lives of youngsters. For parents, comprehending this digital landscape is crucial to guiding their children through the intricacies of growing up in an era dominated by technology. This chapter aims to offer an insight into the current technological milieu, encompassing prominent digital platforms and devices that impact the lives of children and adolescents, along with pertinent statistics and trends reflecting technology usage across various age brackets.

Surveying the Current Technological Scene

The digital realm is characterized by an expansive array of gadgets, platforms, and services that mold how individuals interact, communicate, and consume information. Ranging from smartphones and tablets to social media platforms and online gaming communities, technology pervades nearly every facet of contemporary existence.

Particularly for children and teenagers, digital devices and platforms assume significant roles in their social, educational, and recreational spheres.

Smartphones and tablets

These ubiquitous gadgets have become fixtures in the hands of children and teenagers, offering access to a plethora of apps, games, and online content. Serving as conduits for communication, sources of entertainment, and repositories of educational resources, smartphones and tablets empower users to connect with peers, access information, and participate in various activities while on the move.

Social media platforms

Platforms such as Facebook, Instagram, Snapchat, and TikTok hold immense sway over the younger demographic, providing avenues for social interaction, self-expression, and identity formation. By facilitating the sharing of photos, videos, and messages, these platforms foster connections and communities grounded in shared interests and experiences.

Online Gaming Communities

Online gaming has emerged as a dominant form of entertainment for children and teenagers, with multiplayer titles like Fortnite, Minecraft, and Roblox captivating millions worldwide. These games offer immersive environments where players collaborate, compete, and communicate with one another, forging social bonds and fostering camaraderie.

Streaming Services

Platforms like Netflix, YouTube, and Twitch have revolutionized how youngsters consume media, offering vast libraries of movies, TV shows, and live-streamed content on demand. With personalized recommendations and tailored playlists, these services cater to individual preferences and interests, reshaping the entertainment landscape.

Educational Resources

Technology also plays a pivotal role in education, with online learning platforms, educational apps, and digital textbooks delivering interactive and engaging learning experiences. These resources afford access to educational content around the clock, supplementing traditional classroom instruction and nurturing lifelong learning skills.

Key Digital Platforms and Devices Influencing Children and Teens

The digital panorama is in a perpetual state of flux, with novel platforms and devices continually emerging to shape the experiences of youngsters. Familiarizing oneself with the primary digital platforms and devices that influence this demographic is imperative for parents endeavoring to monitor and regulate their children's online endeavors.

Social media platforms

Platforms like Facebook, Instagram, Snapchat, and TikTok rank among the most frequented destinations for children and teenagers, offering avenues for social interaction, self-expression, and content creation. These platforms facilitate the sharing of photos, videos, and messages, fostering connections and communities rooted in shared interests and experiences.

Messaging Apps

Messaging apps such as WhatsApp, Messenger, and iMessage serve as indispensable communication tools for youngsters, enabling the real-time exchange of text messages, photos, and videos with peers and family members. These apps facilitate convenient and private communication, facilitating group chats and video calls with multiple participants.

Online Gaming Platforms

Platforms like Xbox Live, PlayStation Network, and Steam attract children and teenagers keen on gaming with friends and strangers alike. Offering multiplayer gaming experiences, these platforms enable collaboration, competition, and communication within virtual worlds, fostering social bonds and teamwork skills.

Streaming Services

Major streaming platforms like Netflix, YouTube, and Twitch stand as primary sources of entertainment for children and teenagers, boasting extensive libraries of content available on demand. Through personalized recommendations and curated playlists, these platforms cater to individual preferences and interests, redefining the entertainment landscape.

Educational Apps and Websites

Educational resources such as Khan Academy, Duolingo, and Quizlet provide interactive and stimulating learning experiences for children and teenagers. Encompassing diverse subjects from math and science to languages and the humanities, these resources supplement formal education, providing additional instruction and practice beyond the confines of the classroom.

Parental control tools

For parents seeking to monitor and regulate their children's online activities, parental control tools and software solutions are indispensable. These tools empower parents to impose limits on screen time, block inappropriate content, and monitor their children's digital behavior across devices and platforms, fostering peace of mind in an increasingly interconnected world.

Insights into Statistics and Trends in Technology Usage Across Age Groups

Understanding the statistics and trends in technology usage across various age brackets is crucial for parents' keen on staying abreast of their children's digital habits and behaviors. By delving into data pertaining to device ownership, internet usage, social media engagement, and online activities, parents can glean insights into how technology shapes the lives of children and teenagers.

Device Ownership

Recent studies indicate that the majority of children and teenagers possess smartphones, with ownership rates escalating as they age. While younger children may begin with basic feature phones or tablets, older teenagers are more inclined to wield smartphones boasting advanced features and functionalities.

Internet Usage

Internet usage among children and teenagers is pervasive, with the majority accessing the internet daily for diverse purposes. From perusing social media and indulging in online gaming to conducting educational research and streaming entertainment content, youngsters rely on the internet for a myriad of activities and experiences.

Social media engagement

Teenagers, in particular, exhibit robust engagement with social media platforms like Instagram, Snapchat, and TikTok, dedicating substantial chunks of time to these platforms. Utilizing social media for connecting with friends, sharing content, and exploring interests, teenagers often spend several hours each day scrolling through feeds and interacting with posts.

Online Activities

Children and teenagers partake in a plethora of online activities, spanning social networking, gaming, streaming, and educational pursuits. While some activities foster productivity and enrichment, others entail risks such as cyberbullying, exposure to inappropriate content, and encounters with online predators. Thus, parents must remain vigilant and proactive in monitoring their children's online endeavors to safeguard their well-being.

Digital Well-Being

Concerns regarding digital well-being are increasingly prominent among parents, who harbor apprehensions regarding the adverse ramifications of excessive screen time and online engagement on their children's physical, mental, and emotional health. Studies have uncovered correlations between extensive technology usage and issues like sleep disturbances, academic underperformance, and heightened levels of stress and anxiety.

Conclusion

In summary, grasping the digital landscape is imperative for parents navigating the complexities of raising children in an era dominated by technology. By acquainting themselves with the prominent digital platforms and devices influencing children and teenagers, along with statistics and trends in technology usage across different age groups, parents can better assist their children in cultivating healthy and responsible digital habits. Through proactive monitoring, open communication, and the judicious utilization of parental control tools, parents can empower their children to navigate the digital realm safely and confidently.

Chapter 3

Early Childhood and Technology

The Role of Technology in Early Childhood Development

The formative years of a child's life are pivotal for cognitive, social, emotional, and physical growth. Technology, when used appropriately, can aid in fostering this development. However, it's imperative to grasp both the potential advantages and the hurdles involved in integrating technology into early childhood experiences.

Cognitive Development: Interactive digital platforms like educational apps and games have the capacity to spark cognitive development in young children. These platforms can introduce fundamental concepts in mathematics, language, and science through captivating and interactive content. For instance, apps that teach alphabet recognition, counting, and problem-solving can boost early literacy and numeracy skills.

Social and Emotional Development: Technology can also bolster social and emotional growth. Video chat platforms like Skype or FaceTime facilitate young children in maintaining relationships with distant family members, fostering social connections, and developing communication skills. Some apps are designed to impart lessons in emotional regulation and empathy through storytelling and interactive scenarios.

Motor Skills Development: Certain digital activities can aid in refining fine motor skills. Apps that involve dragging, tapping, or drawing can enhance hand-eye coordination and dexterity. Nonetheless, it's crucial to strike a balance between screen time and physical activities that promote gross motor skills, such as running, jumping, and climbing.

Language Development: Exposure to language via digital media can facilitate language acquisition. Educational programs and apps that incorporate storytelling, songs, and interactive dialogues can enrich vocabulary and comprehension skills. Parents can utilize technology as a tool to introduce new languages or reinforce native language skills.

Creativity and Imagination: Digital tools have the potential to ignite creativity and imagination. Drawing apps, music creation software, and digital storytelling platforms enable children to express themselves artistically. These tools can complement traditional creative activities like painting, building with blocks, and imaginative play.

Educational Apps and Screen Time Recommendations for Toddlers

While technology can provide educational benefits, it's vital to use it judiciously, especially with toddlers. The American Academy of Pediatrics (AAP) offers guidelines for screen time to ensure that young children maintain a balanced and healthy relationship with technology.

Screen Time Recommendations:

1. **Under 18 months:** It's advisable to refrain from using screen media except for video chatting. Parents should engage in interactive play and reading with their infants instead.
2. **18–24 Months:** If parents opt to introduce digital media, it should consist of high-quality content, and parents should actively watch and

engage with their children to aid their comprehension.

3. **2 to 5 Years:** Limit screen time to one hour per day of high-quality programming. Co-viewing with parents is recommended to help children grasp and apply what they learn to their surroundings. Choosing Educational Apps: When selecting educational apps for toddlers, parents should consider the following criteria:

4. **Age-appropriate Content:** Apps should cater to the developmental stage of toddlers, featuring simple interfaces and activities aligned with their cognitive and motor skills.

5. **Educational Value:** Look for apps that impart fundamental concepts such as numbers, letters, shapes, colors, and basic problem-solving skills.

6. **Interactive Engagement:** Opt for apps that necessitate active participation rather than passive consumption. Interactive features like touch, drag-and-drop, and voice commands can enhance learning.

7. **Parental Involvement:** Choose apps that encourage interaction between parent and child. Jointly playing and

discussing the app's content can reinforce learning and deepen the child's understanding.

8. **Positive Content:** Ensure that the app promotes positive messages and behaviors, avoiding any violent or inappropriate content. Recommended Educational Apps for Toddlers:

9. Endless Alphabet is an interactive app that aids children in learning letters and expanding their vocabulary through playful animations and phonics games.

10. **PBS Kids Video:** Grants access to educational videos featuring beloved PBS characters like Daniel Tiger and Sesame Street, designed to impart social skills, problem-solving abilities, and basic academic concepts.

11. Sago Mini World offers a range of creative play activities that stimulate imagination and storytelling through exploration and discovery.

12. ABCmouse is a comprehensive early learning app covering reading, math, art, and music through engaging games and activities tailored to different age levels.

Balancing Technology with Traditional Play and Learning Methods

While technology can serve as a valuable educational tool, it's crucial to strike a balance between digital activities and traditional play and learning methods. Traditional play is essential for a child's holistic development, fostering physical, social, and cognitive skills that digital media alone cannot provide.

Encouraging Physical Activity: Physical activity is essential for developing gross motor skills, coordination, and overall health. Parents should ensure that toddlers engage in plenty of active play, such as running, climbing, and playing with balls. Outdoor activities like visits to the park, nature walks, and playground play offer vital physical exercise and exposure to nature.

Fostering Social Interaction: Social interactions are paramount for developing communication and social skills. Encourage playdates and group activities where children can interact with peers, learn to share, take turns, and develop empathy. Cooperative games and role-playing scenarios can aid children in understanding social dynamics and forming relationships.

Promoting Creative Play: Creative play stimulates imagination and problem-solving skills. Provide children with materials for open-ended play, such as building blocks, art supplies, and dress-up costumes. Activities like drawing, painting, and building encourage self-expression and innovation.

Integrating Sensory Play: Sensory play engages a child's senses and supports cognitive and physical development. Activities like playing with sand, water, playdough, and sensory bins allow children to explore textures, shapes, and colors. Sensory play can also be soothing and therapeutic, helping children regulate their emotions.

Reading and Storytelling: Reading books and storytelling are crucial for language development and literacy skills. Parents should read to their children daily, selecting age-appropriate books that capture their interest and imagination. Interactive storytelling, where children participate in creating or retelling stories, can enhance comprehension and creativity.

Setting a Routine: Establishing a daily routine that encompasses a balance of digital and traditional activities can help children develop healthy habits. Allocate specific times for screen time, physical play, creative activities, and quiet time for reading and rest. Consistency and structure provide a sense of security and predictability for young children.

Parental Involvement: Active parental involvement is key to maximizing the benefits of both digital and traditional play. Parents should engage with their children during digital activities, posing questions and encouraging discussion about what they're learning. Similarly, participating in traditional play activities strengthens the parent-child bond and offers opportunities for teaching and guidance.

Conclusion

Incorporating technology into early childhood development necessitates a thoughtful and balanced approach. While digital devices and educational apps can offer significant benefits, they should complement rather than replace traditional play and learning methods. By adhering to screen time recommendations, selecting high-quality educational apps, and fostering an environment rich in physical, social, and creative activities, parents can support their children's holistic development in an era driven by technology. Active parental involvement and the establishment of a balanced routine are crucial for helping young children navigate the digital world while reaping the full benefits of both digital and traditional play.

Chapter 4

Navigating Technology Throughout Schooling

As technology evolves, its incorporation into elementary education becomes increasingly essential. This section delves into effectively integrating technology into young learners' educational settings, emphasizing cyber safety, digital literacy, and methods for managing screen time and fostering healthy online behaviors.

Integrating Technology in Primary Education

Incorporating technology into elementary education yields numerous advantages, including heightened engagement, tailored learning experiences, and enriched access to educational materials. Modern classrooms boast various digital tools, from interactive whiteboards and tablets to educational software and online learning platforms.

Interactive Whiteboards: Interactive whiteboards have transformed traditional teaching by enabling educators to craft dynamic, multimedia lessons. These boards showcase videos, animations, and interactive diagrams, amplifying engagement and facilitating real-time collaboration and problem-solving.

Tablets and laptops: Many schools furnish students with tablets or laptops, fostering personalized learning journeys. These devices grant access to a plethora of digital resources, including e-books, educational apps, and online research tools, promoting a blend of independent and collaborative learning.

Educational Software and Apps: Tailored educational software and apps reinforce curriculum concepts through interactive games and activities. Platforms like ABCmouse, Starfall, and Khan Academy offer subject-specific lessons, making learning enjoyable and accessible.

Online Learning Platforms: Platforms such as Google Classroom, Seesaw, and Edmodo streamline assignment management and facilitate communication between educators, students, and parents. These platforms also enable multimedia integration and access to assignments from anywhere.

STEM Education and Coding: Integrating STEM education into elementary curricula is vital for preparing students for the future. Coding classes and robotics programs introduce foundational programming and problem-solving skills, fostering critical thinking and creativity.

Benefits of Technology Integration

1. **Enhanced Engagement:** Multimedia lessons capture students' attention, enhancing learning experiences.
2. **Personalized Learning:** Technology facilitates tailored instruction, accommodating diverse learning styles and paces.
3. **Access to Resources:** Digital tools offer instant access to a wealth of educational materials.
4. **Collaboration and Communication:** Technology fosters collaboration among students and strengthens communication between educators, students, and parents.
5. **Skill Development:** Students cultivate essential digital literacy skills crucial for academic and career success.

Challenges of Technology Integration:

1. **Equity and Access:** Ensuring universal access to technology, particularly in underserved communities, poses a significant challenge.
2. **Teacher Training:** Effective integration necessitates ongoing professional development to keep educators abreast of evolving tools and practices.
3. **Screen Time Management:** Balancing screen time with traditional learning and physical activities is crucial for students' overall well-being.

Cyber Safety and Digital Literacy for Children

As children engage more with digital technologies, teaching cyber safety and digital literacy becomes imperative. Educating children about safe online practices and responsible digital behavior is essential for safeguarding them and fostering positive online experiences.

Understanding Cyber Safety: Cyber safety entails measures to protect children from online threats like cyberbullying and exposure to inappropriate content. Collaborative efforts between educators and parents are crucial in establishing a secure online environment.

Key Cyber Safety Practices:

1. **Protect Personal Information:** Instruct children not to divulge personal details to strangers online.
2. **Safe Social Media Use:** Educate children on privacy settings and the risks of oversharing on social platforms.
3. **Recognizing Cyberbullying:** Help children identify and report cyberbullying incidents.
4. **Avoiding Online Strangers:** Emphasize the dangers of interacting with unfamiliar individuals online.
5. **Secure Passwords:** Teach children to create and safeguard strong passwords.

Digital Literacy Education: Digital literacy encompasses navigating the digital realm safely and effectively, including using digital tools, evaluating online information critically, and practicing responsible online behavior.

Key Components of Digital Literacy:

1. Technical Skills: Basic competency in using digital devices and software.
2. Information literacy is the ability to discern credible sources and avoid misinformation.
3. Online Etiquette: Understanding appropriate online behavior and communication norms.
4. Digital Footprint: Awareness of the lasting impact of online actions.
5. Critical Thinking: Encouraging skepticism and discernment when consuming digital content.

Resources for Teaching Cyber Safety and Digital Literacy: Platforms like Common Sense Media, NetSmartz, and Be Internet Awesome offer educational materials and activities to promote internet safety and digital citizenship.

Managing Screen Time and Cultivating Healthy Online Habits

Balancing screen time with other activities is crucial for children's well-being. While technology can be beneficial, excessive screen time can have adverse effects on physical and mental health and academic performance.

Recommended Screen Time Guidelines: Follow guidelines established by the American Academy of Pediatrics to ensure a healthy balance of screen time for different age groups.

Strategies for Managing Screen Time:

1. Set Clear Boundaries: Establish rules for screen use and designate screen-free zones.
2. Encourage Alternative Activities: Promote non-digital activities like outdoor play and reading.
3. Model healthy behavior: Lead by example by managing your own screen time.
4. Create a Screen Time Schedule: Develop a consistent schedule for screen use, homework, and other activities.
5. Use Parental Control Tools: Employ parental controls to monitor and limit screen time and content.

Promoting Healthy Online Habits:

1. **Balance Screen Time with Physical Activity:** Encourage regular exercise to counterbalance sedentary screen time.
2. **Monitor Content Quality:** Choose educational content aligned with children's interests.
3. **Foster Social Interaction:** Support face-to-face interactions and social skill development.
4. **Prioritize sleep:** Establish a bedtime routine free from screens.
5. **Engage in Co-Viewing:** Watch and discuss digital content with children to guide their online experiences.

The Role of Schools in Managing Screen Time:

Educators play a pivotal role in promoting healthy screen habits and integrating technology into the curriculum responsibly. Schools should balance digital and traditional teaching methods and involve parents in promoting healthy screen habits at home.

Conclusion

Navigating technology in education requires a balanced approach. While integrating technology offers substantial benefits, it also poses challenges, such as ensuring equitable access and managing screen time. Teaching cyber safety and digital literacy is vital for protecting children online, while fostering healthy screen habits is essential for their overall well-being. By promoting a balanced approach to technology use, educators and parents can equip children with the skills and habits needed for success in the digital age.

Chapter 5

Adolescents and Social Media

In the contemporary era, social media holds considerable sway over the lives of teenagers. This chapter delves into how social media influences teenage identity and self-esteem, tackles the hurdles of cyberbullying and online peer pressure, and provides strategies for fostering responsible social media usage among adolescents.

The Impact of Social Media on Adolescent Identity and Self-Esteem

Identity Formation: Adolescence is a phase marked by profound self-exploration and identity-shaping. Social media platforms offer avenues for teenagers to delve into and express their identities, connect with peers who share similar interests and values, and seek validation from others.

Carefully Crafted Image: Social media prompts teenagers to meticulously curate their online personas, highlighting aspects of their lives they wish to showcase while concealing their vulnerabilities. This curated image creation can induce pressure to conform to unrealistic standards of beauty, success, and popularity.

Comparisons and Envy: Exposure to idealized images and lifestyles on social media can incite teenagers to unfavorably compare themselves to their peers, fostering feelings of inadequacy and envy. Continuously encountering edited photos, lavish vacations, and seemingly flawless relationships can distort teenagers' perceptions of reality and contribute to diminished self-esteem.

Validation Seeking: Likes, comments, and followers serve as social currency on social media, reinforcing the craving for external validation and approval. Teenagers may gauge their self-worth based on the reception their posts receive, fostering a dependence on external validation for self-esteem.

Impact on Self-Esteem: Studies indicate a correlation between social media usage and adverse psychological effects like depression, anxiety, and low self-esteem among teenagers. Excessive time spent on social media can exacerbate feelings of loneliness, isolation, and discontentment with one's own life.

Promoting Healthy Self-Esteem Practices: Nurturing a healthy sense of self-esteem in the digital age necessitates cultivating self-awareness, resilience, and self-acceptance among teenagers. Parents, educators, and caregivers can aid teenagers by:

Encouraging Authenticity: Embracing uniqueness and authenticity should be encouraged both online and offline. Teenagers should be reminded that being themselves is perfectly acceptable, and they are deserving of love and acceptance as they are.

Limiting Social Comparisons: Adolescents should be guided to restrict exposure to idealized images and lifestyles on social media. They need to understand that people often only portray the highlights of their lives online and that everyone encounters challenges and setbacks.

Fostering Real-World Connections: Encouraging meaningful offline relationships and interactions is crucial. Engaging in activities that facilitate face-to-face interaction, such as family dinners, team sports, clubs, and volunteer work, can be beneficial.

Developing Resilience: Equipping teenagers with coping mechanisms for handling setbacks, criticism, and rejection is essential. They need to comprehend that failure is a natural aspect of life and an opportunity for growth and learning.

Modeling Healthy Behavior: Adults should exemplify healthy self-esteem and responsible social media usage. Negative comments about one's appearance or comparisons with others online should be avoided.

Addressing cyberbullying and online peer pressure

Cyberbullying: Cyberbullying entails using digital platforms to harass, intimidate, or humiliate others, taking forms like spreading rumors or posting hurtful content. It can have severe repercussions for victims, including depression, anxiety, and suicidal thoughts.

Online Peer Pressure: Social media magnifies the impact of peer pressure by perpetuating constant social comparisons and judgments. Teenagers may feel compelled to conform to certain standards to gain acceptance, leading to risky behaviors and unhealthy habits.

Strategies for Tackling Cyberbullying and Online Peer Pressure:

Open Communication: Establishing a supportive environment where teenagers feel comfortable discussing their online experiences is crucial. Encourage them to report instances of cyberbullying and peer pressure to a trusted adult.

Educating About Online Safety: Teenagers should be educated about the risks associated with sharing personal information online and the importance of privacy settings. They need to understand the consequences of cyberbullying and online harassment.

Empowering Bystanders: Encourage teenagers to intervene when they witness cyberbullying or online peer pressure. Teach them how to support victims and stand against negative behavior.

Promoting Digital Empathy: Fostering empathy and compassion is essential. Teenagers should be made aware of the

impact of their online actions and encouraged to consider the consequences of their content.

Seeking Professional Help: If cyberbullying or online peer pressure negatively impacts a teenager's mental health, seeking assistance from a mental health professional or school counselor is vital.

Encouraging Responsible Social Media Usage

Establishing Guidelines: Clear guidelines and expectations regarding social media usage, including rules on content and screen time limits, should be set. Teenagers should be involved in the development of these rules to ensure understanding and compliance.

Modeling Positive Behavior: Adults should demonstrate responsible social media use and digital citizenship. They should show teenagers how to engage in respectful online communication and utilize social media for positive self-expression and connection.

Monitoring and supervision: Regularly discussing teenagers' online activities and monitoring their social media accounts is important. Open communication should be encouraged, and support should be readily available.

Teaching Critical Thinking: Teenagers should be equipped with critical thinking skills to discern the credibility of online information. They need to learn to identify misinformation and verify information from multiple sources.

Promoting Positive Content: Encouraging teenagers to share uplifting content that inspires and educates others is beneficial. Following accounts that promote diversity, inclusion, and social justice can broaden perspectives.

Encouraging Offline Activities: Balancing social media use with offline activities is essential for overall well-being. Teenagers should be encouraged to pursue hobbies, spend time with loved ones, and engage in activities that nourish their holistic development.

Building Digital Resilience: Teenagers should be taught how to navigate online challenges with resilience. Seeking support from trusted individuals, practicing self-care, and maintaining a healthy perspective on social media are valuable skills.

Conclusion

Navigating social media during adolescence presents both opportunities and challenges for teenagers and their caregivers. By promoting responsible social media usage, fostering open communication, and teaching critical thinking and digital resilience, adults can empower teenagers to navigate the digital realm confidently and responsibly. Equipping teenagers with the necessary skills and support enables them to harness the positive potential of social media while mitigating its risks.

Chapter 6

Technology's Impact on Mental Well-Being

In the contemporary era, technology has seamlessly integrated into our daily lives, especially for young people. While it offers manifold advantages such as access to information, social interaction, and entertainment, excessive usage can detrimentally affect mental health. This chapter delves into the correlation between screen time and mental well-being, identifies indicators of technology dependency and digital exhaustion, and proposes methods to foster digital wellness among adolescents.

Exploring the Relationship Between Screen Time and Mental Health

The link between screen time and mental health has become a growing concern among various stakeholders. Despite the benefits technology provides in terms of education, communication, and leisure, prolonged screen exposure has been associated with a spectrum of mental health issues like depression, anxiety, and diminished overall welfare.

Social media's influence on mental health

Social media platforms wield significant influence over adolescents' social interactions and self-perception. Studies demonstrate a connection between heavy social media usage and adverse mental health outcomes, including diminished self-esteem, feelings of isolation, and depressive tendencies. The constant barrage of curated images and idealized lifestyles fosters feelings of inadequacy and social comparison.

Disruption of Sleep Patterns

Excessive screen time, particularly before bedtime, disrupts sleep cycles and compromises overall well-being. The blue light emitted by screens inhibits melatonin production, making it difficult to fall and stay asleep. Poor sleep quality is linked to various mental health issues, such as depression, anxiety, and irritability.

Cyberbullying and online harassment

Cyberbullying and online harassment pose significant threats in the digital realm, profoundly impacting mental health. Individuals subjected to online harassment experience fear, shame, and social exclusion, elevating the risk of depression, anxiety, and suicidal thoughts.

Virtual reality and immersive technologies

Emerging technologies like virtual reality offer novel avenues for entertainment but raise concerns about their psychological impact. While VR experiences are captivating, excessive indulgence may blur the boundary between reality and fantasy, leading to detachment from real-world relationships and obligations.

Identifying Signs of Technology Addiction and Digital Burnout

Technology Addiction: Characterized by compulsive and excessive digital device usage despite adverse consequences, technology addiction manifests through preoccupation with technology, neglect of personal hygiene, and difficulty controlling usage.

Digital Burnout: Digital burnout emerges when individuals feel overwhelmed and emotionally drained by their digital engagements. Symptoms include stress, difficulty concentrating, physical ailments, decreased productivity, and social withdrawal.

Impact on Mental Health

Technology addiction and digital burnout exert profound ramifications on mental well-being, fostering anxiety, depression, and social isolation. Moreover, excessive digital engagement impedes daily functioning, relationships, and academic or professional performance.

Strategies to Promote Digital Wellness in Adolescents

Establishing Boundaries: Implement clear guidelines regarding technology usage, including designated screen-free periods and spaces. Encourage breaks from screens and engagement in offline activities.

Encouraging Mindful Technology Usage:
Advocate for intentional and mindful technology consumption, prompting reflection on digital habits and prioritizing activities fostering joy, fulfillment, and connection.

Modeling Healthy Behavior: Set a positive example by balancing screen time with offline pursuits, such as outdoor activities and face-to-face interactions.

Promoting Digital Detoxes: Facilitate periodic technology breaks to recharge and reconnect with nature and loved ones.

Teaching Coping Mechanisms: Equip adolescents with coping strategies to manage stress and emotions without technology, such as mindfulness practices and deep breathing exercises.

Fostering Offline Connections: Encourage meaningful offline relationships and social interactions to counterbalance digital engagement.

Promoting Digital Literacy: Educate adolescents on critical thinking to discern online content and navigate the digital landscape responsibly.

Encouraging Physical Activity: Advocate for physical exercise as an alternative to screen time to promote physical and mental well-being.

Educating on Online Safety: Provide guidance on online safety and responsible digital citizenship, emphasizing the risks of sharing personal information and interacting with strangers.

Seeking Professional Help: When technology negatively impacts mental health, seek assistance from mental health professionals to develop coping mechanisms and healthy habits.

Conclusion

While technology enriches the lives of adolescents, excessive screen time and digital saturation pose risks to mental health. By recognizing indicators of technology addiction and digital burnout and implementing strategies to foster digital wellness, caregivers can navigate the digital landscape responsibly. Balancing technology use with offline activities promotes the holistic development and mental well-being of the younger generation.

Chapter 7

Managing Children's Online Safety and Privacy

In today's digital landscape, parents must find the right balance between ensuring their children's safety online and respecting their privacy. Parental controls and monitoring tools offer solutions to address these concerns effectively. This chapter gives an overview of the available technologies, advice on setting up effective monitoring and filtering systems, and strategies for maintaining a healthy balance between supervision and privacy in the digital era.

An Overview of Parental Control Technologies

1. **Device-Based Controls:** These are features or apps embedded in devices like smartphones, tablets, and computers. They enable parents to manage and limit their children's device usage, block inappropriate content and apps, control privacy settings, and monitor online activities. Examples include Apple's

Screen Time, Google Family Link, and Microsoft Family Safety.

2. **Router-Based Controls:** Operating at the network level, these controls manage internet access for all devices connected to the home network. They offer features like content filtering, time-based restrictions, and device-specific controls. Examples include Netgear Circle, OpenDNS Family Shield, and Gryphon Guardian.

3. **Third-Party Monitoring Apps:** These apps provide additional features for parents who want comprehensive control over their children's online activities. Features include real-time monitoring, location tracking, and remote management. Examples include Qustodio, Bark, and the Norton family.

Setting up effective monitoring and filtering systems

1. **Assess Your Needs:** Understand your family's specific needs, values, and concerns regarding online safety and privacy before implementing controls.

2. **Choose Tools Wisely:** Select tools that match your family's needs, considering compatibility, ease of use, and available features.
3. **Establish Clear Rules:** Communicate clear rules and expectations regarding online behavior, privacy, and consequences for rule violations.
4. **Customize Settings:** Tailor settings and restrictions based on your children's age, interests, and maturity level.
5. **Educate Your Children:** Explain the purpose of controls and encourage open communication about online experiences.
6. **Monitor Activity:** Regularly review activity reports to stay informed about your children's online activities.
7. **Maintain Communication:** Keep communication channels open and encourage your children to discuss any concerns they may have.

Balancing privacy and supervision

1. **Respect Privacy:** Respect your child's privacy while prioritizing their safety.

2. **Gradually Increase Independence:** Grant more independence as your children demonstrate responsible online behavior.
3. **Foster Trust**: Build trust through open communication and non-judgmental support.
4. **Use Monitoring as a Teaching Tool:** Use monitoring as an opportunity to teach digital literacy and responsible behavior.
5. **Model Healthy Habits:** Lead by example by demonstrating healthy digital habits.
6. **Adapt Over Time:** Be flexible and adapt your approach as your children grow and their digital habits change.

Conclusion

Parental controls and monitoring tools are essential for navigating the digital world responsibly. By selecting the right tools, setting clear guidelines, and balancing supervision with privacy, parents can create a safe online environment for their children. Through open communication and trust-building, parents can empower their children to navigate the digital world confidently and responsibly.

Chapter 8

Digital Citizenship and Ethics

In the age of digital dominance, it's crucial to educate youngsters on responsible online conduct and ethical awareness. Digital citizenship encompasses a spectrum of abilities and principles that empower individuals to engage safely, ethically, and conscientiously in the digital realm. This chapter delves into the significance of educating children about digital footprints and online reputation, fostering values of empathy and respect in online interactions, and addressing issues of digital piracy and plagiarism.

Educating Children About Digital Footprints and Online Reputation

Understanding Digital Footprints: The digital footprint refers to the trace of data individuals leave behind while using digital platforms and devices, including social media posts, online comments, search history, and shared personal data. Teaching kids about digital footprints helps them grasp the idea of permanence and the potential impact of their online actions on their reputation and future prospects.

Managing Online Reputation: Online reputation pertains to how individuals are perceived based on their digital footprint. Children need to comprehend that their online behavior can significantly influence their reputation, both personally and professionally. Encouraging critical thinking regarding the content they share online and its potential perception by others is essential. They should learn to proactively manage their online presence by adjusting privacy settings, contemplating before posting, and showcasing positive aspects of their interests and achievements online.

Educating on Online Safety: Teaching children about online safety and privacy is crucial to managing their digital footprint. Discussing the risks associated with sharing personal information online, interacting with strangers, and engaging in risky behaviors is important. Children should be encouraged to exercise caution online and report any instances of cyberbullying or online harassment to a trusted adult.

Instilling Values of Empathy and Respect in Online Interactions

Promoting digital empathy: Empathy is pivotal in fostering positive and respectful online interactions. Children should be taught to practice digital empathy by considering the impact of their words and actions on others, standing up against cyberbullying, and promoting kindness and inclusion in online communities.

Responsible Social Media Use: While social media platforms offer avenues for self-expression and connection, children should be educated about responsible usage, respecting others' privacy and boundaries, thinking critically about shared content, respecting diverse opinions, and managing screen time effectively.

Navigating Issues of Digital Piracy and Plagiarism

Understanding Digital Piracy: Digital piracy involves the unauthorized use of copyrighted materials. Children should learn about its ethical and legal implications and be encouraged to support creators by obtaining content through legal means.

Preventing Plagiarism: Plagiarism occurs when individuals use someone else's work without proper attribution. Children should understand the importance of academic integrity, learn to cite sources properly, express their own ideas, and develop critical thinking skills to evaluate online information.

Promoting Digital Literacy: Digital literacy is indispensable for responsibly navigating the digital world. Children should be taught to critically evaluate online information, distinguish between credible and unreliable sources, and verify information from multiple sources.

Conclusion

Digital citizenship and ethics are foundational for enabling children to navigate the digital world safely, responsibly, and ethically. By educating children about digital footprints, fostering values of empathy and respect, and addressing issues of digital piracy and plagiarism, parents and educators can equip them with the necessary skills and values to thrive in the digital age, fostering a culture of responsibility and ethical behavior online.

Chapter 9

The Impact of Technology on Education

The educational landscape has been revolutionized by technology, ushering in new avenues for learning, collaboration, and creativity. This chapter delves into the emergence of e-learning and virtual classrooms, the effective utilization of educational technology to bolster learning achievements, and strategies for navigating the blend of online and offline learning in today's digital era.

The Emergence of E-Learning and Virtual Classrooms

1. Evolution of E-Learning: E-learning, denoting the utilization of digital tools to disseminate educational content and facilitate learning beyond traditional classroom confines, has witnessed remarkable growth lately. This surge is fueled by technological advancements and a growing demand for flexible and accessible learning

avenues. Key advancements in e-learning encompass:

- o **Online courses and MOOCs (Massive Open Online Courses):** Platforms like Coursera, edX, and Khan Academy provide a plethora of courses across various subjects, accessible globally.
- o **Virtual classrooms and web conferencing:** Tools such as Zoom, Google Meet, and Microsoft Teams enable real-time collaboration and interaction between educators and learners in virtual settings.
- o **Learning management systems (LMS):** Platforms like Moodle, Canvas, and Blackboard serve as centralized hubs for managing course materials, assignments, and communication between instructors and students.

1. **Advantages of E-Learning:** E-learning brings forth myriad benefits

for educators and learners alike, including:

- o **Flexibility and accessibility:** Learners can access educational content and engage in learning activities from any location with internet connectivity, catering to diverse needs and schedules.
- o **Personalized learning experiences:** E-learning platforms often integrate adaptive learning technologies, tailoring instruction and content to individual learners' needs, preferences, and learning styles.
- o **Collaboration and interaction:** Virtual classrooms and online forums facilitate collaboration, peer-to-peer learning, and knowledge exchange.
- o **Cost-effectiveness:** E-learning proves to be more cost-effective compared to traditional classroom setups, reducing expenses tied to

travel, materials, and infrastructure maintenance.

1. **Challenges of E-Learning:** Despite its advantages, e-learning presents challenges and considerations for both educators and learners, including:

   o **Technical hurdles and digital disparities:** Unequal access to internet connectivity, digital devices, and technical assistance can impede e-learning for students in underserved or rural areas, necessitating efforts to bridge the digital gap.

   o **Engagement and motivation:** Sustaining student engagement and motivation in online environments can be daunting, especially for younger students or those lacking self-regulation skills, requiring effective instructional strategies and technologies to foster active participation.

- o **Social and emotional aspects:** E-learning may lack the social interactions and sense of community inherent in traditional classrooms, potentially affecting students' social and emotional well-being, highlighting the need for strategies to nurture social connections and support socio-emotional development.

Leveraging Educational Technology for Enhanced Learning

1. **Blended Learning Approaches:** Blended learning amalgamates traditional face-to-face instruction with online learning activities, offering a flexible and personalized educational approach. These models, characterized by a mix of in-person and online elements, cater to diverse learner needs and preferences.
2. **Interactive and Multimedia Resources:** Educational technology tools like interactive simulations, virtual labs, and multimedia presentations enrich learning

experiences by providing immersive and engaging content. These resources facilitate exploration of complex concepts, visualization of abstract ideas, and interactive engagement with content, accommodating diverse learning styles.

3. **Gamification and Game-Based Learning:** Gamification entails integrating game elements into educational activities to enhance engagement and learning outcomes. Game-based learning employs educational games as primary instructional tools, fostering collaboration, competition, and intrinsic motivation among students.

4. **Adaptive Learning Technologies:** Adaptive learning technologies leverage algorithms and data analytics to personalize instruction and adapt learning experiences to individual learners needs. These technologies support differentiated instruction, assist struggling learners, and challenge advanced students, ultimately improving learning outcomes for all.

5. **Collaboration and Communication Tools:** Technology tools like online

discussion forums and video conferencing platforms facilitate communication and collaboration among teachers and students in virtual environments. These tools promote active learning, critical thinking, and social interaction, essential skills in the digital age.

Balancing online and offline learning

1. **Establish Clear Learning Objectives:** Align instructional activities with clear learning objectives and educational goals, striking a balance between online and offline activities to create cohesive learning experiences.
2. **Provide Hands-On Learning Opportunities:** Integrate hands-on experiences and real-world applications into the curriculum to complement online learning and foster active, experiential learning.
3. **Cultivate Self-Regulation Skills:** Teach students self-regulation skills and strategies to manage their time, attention, and digital behavior effectively, fostering habits of self-

directed learning and responsible technology use.

4. **Promote Digital Wellness:** Educate students about maintaining a healthy balance between online and offline activities, encouraging breaks from screens, physical activity, and hobbies outside of technology.

5. **Emphasize Social and Emotional Learning:** Integrate social and emotional learning activities into the curriculum to support students' socio-emotional development and well-being, creating a supportive and inclusive learning environment.

Conclusion

Technology has reshaped education, providing new avenues for learning, collaboration, and innovation. By embracing e-learning and virtual classrooms, leveraging educational technology to enhance learning outcomes, and effectively managing the balance between online and offline learning, educators can create engaging, personalized, and effective learning experiences for students.

Chapter 10

Nurturing Creativity and Innovation

In the modern era, cultivating creativity and innovation is paramount for success, particularly among youngsters. Technology stands as a potent ally in this endeavor, serving to both ignite creativity and foster innovative thinking in children. This chapter delves into the pivotal role of technology in nurturing creativity, utilizing coding, robotics, and other tech-oriented activities to spur imagination while also advocating for problem-solving and critical thinking through hands-on tech initiatives.

Utilizing technology to spark creativity in children

1. **Innovative Tools and Software:** Technology provides an extensive array of tools and applications that empower children to express themselves and explore their creative potential. Ranging from digital art and music composition software to video editing and animation tools,

these applications offer boundless avenues for creative expression and experimentation. Encouraging children to explore various mediums and discover tools that resonate with their interests and skills is vital.

2. **Digital Storytelling and Multimedia Endeavors:** Digital storytelling and multimedia ventures blend traditional storytelling techniques with digital tools, resulting in captivating narratives. Children can utilize platforms like Adobe Spark, Storybird, or Scratch to craft their own stories, poems, or comics. Encouraging exploration of diverse storytelling formats, such as podcasts or interactive multimedia presentations, fosters creativity and facilitates sharing creations with others.

3. **Maker Culture and DIY Initiatives:** The maker movement champions experiential learning through hands-on DIY projects, merging technology with art, engineering, and design. Maker spaces equipped with tools like 3D printers and microcontrollers provide environments for children to innovate and create their own inventions.

Encouraging a maker mindset enables the exploration of projects that blend technology with various disciplines, nurturing creativity and problem-solving skills.

4. **Augmented and Virtual Realities:** Augmented reality (AR) and virtual reality (VR) technologies offer immersive experiences bridging the physical and digital realms. Children can use AR and VR applications to explore virtual environments and create their own experiences. Encouraging experimentation with tools like Tilt Brush or CoSpaces Edu allows children to showcase their creativity through 3D artwork or interactive stories.

Coding, Robotics, and Tech-Centric Creative Pursuits

1. **Coding and Programming:** Learning to code empowers children to become creators of technology, fostering problem-solving and creative expression. Introducing coding concepts through projects combining coding with storytelling or

game design facilitates critical thinking and self-expression.

2. **Robotics and Engineering:** Robotics projects integrate creativity, design thinking, and technical skills, enabling children to build and program robots. Hands-on activities with robotics kits like LEGO Mindstorms instill problem-solving abilities, while programming languages such as Blockly or Arduino bring creations to life.

3. **Digital Music and Sound Design:** Digital audio workstations and music composition software provide platforms for children to explore music production and sound design. Experimentation with different genres and production techniques fosters creativity and artistic expression.

4. **Game Design and Development:** Game design platforms like Scratch or Unity empower children to create interactive games, nurturing creativity and computational thinking skills. Exploring game mechanics and storytelling enhances problem-solving abilities.

Fostering Problem-Solving and Critical Thinking Through Tech Projects

1. **Project-Based Learning:** Engaging children in project-based learning experiences integrates technology to address real-world problems, fostering critical thinking and collaboration skills.

2. **Design Thinking Process:** Applying the design thinking process encourages children to empathize, ideate, prototype, and iterate, fostering innovative solutions across various domains.

3. **Computational Thinking Skills:** Teaching computational thinking skills through coding activities enables children to analyze problems and devise solutions using logical reasoning and algorithms.

4. **Reflective Practice:** Encouraging reflective practice throughout the creative process promotes learning and growth. Documenting progress and receiving feedback fosters continuous improvement.

Conclusion

Technology serves as a catalyst for creativity and innovation, empowering children to become creators and problem-solvers in the digital age. By leveraging technology to inspire creativity, introducing coding, robotics, and other tech-driven activities, and nurturing problem-solving and critical thinking through hands-on projects, educators and parents can prepare children to thrive in a complex and interconnected world where their ideas shape the future.

Chapter 11

Family Interactions in a Technology-Infused Household

In today's digitally dominated society, families encounter distinct challenges and advantages as they manage the blend of technology and family life. This chapter delves into approaches for establishing areas and periods in the home free from technology, utilizing technology to reinforce familial bonds, and resolving conflicts related to technology to cultivate a positive and equitable family dynamic in the era of digitalization.

Creating Tech-Free Zones and Times in the Household

1. **Setting Limits**: Clearly defining boundaries regarding technology usage is vital for maintaining equilibrium and harmony at home. Designate specific spaces like the dining or living area as tech-free zones, encouraging face-to-face interactions. Introduce tech-free

periods during meals, before bedtime, or on designated family nights to promote undistracted quality time and meaningful connections.

2. **Regulating Screen Time:** Imposing restrictions on screen time for both children and adults helps curb excessive technology use and promote healthier habits. Utilize parental control tools or screen time management apps to set daily or weekly limits on device usage for each family member. Encourage alternative activities such as outdoor play, reading, or creative hobbies during screen-free periods to enhance physical, mental, and emotional well-being.

3. **Leading by Example:** Parents serve as crucial role models for demonstrating healthy technology habits and behaviors to their children. Exhibit responsible screen usage by limiting your own screen time, prioritizing face-to-face interactions, and engaging in offline activities together as a family. Create opportunities for meaningful connections and quality time sans screens, such as family dinners, game nights, or outdoor excursions, to

underscore the importance of balance and moderation in technology use.

4. **Establishing Tech-Free Traditions:** Incorporate tech-free rituals and routines into your family's daily schedule to foster moments of connection and presence. Initiate or conclude each day with a tech-free activity, such as sharing highlights from the day, practicing mindfulness, or reading together. Utilize these tech-free rituals as occasions to bond, communicate, and strengthen family relationships away from the distractions of screens and devices.

Utilizing Technology to Enhance Family Bonds

1. **Family Game Nights:** Family game nights offer opportunities for bonding, laughter, and friendly competition in a technology-centric household. Opt for a variety of board games, card games, or digital games catering to diverse interests and age groups within the family. Consider integrating digital games that promote teamwork, problem-solving, and creativity to foster positive

interactions and communication skills among family members.

2. **Shared Online Activities:** Technology can serve as a catalyst for uniting families through shared online activities and experiences. Explore virtual events, workshops, or classes aligned with your family's interests, such as cooking classes or virtual museum tours. Engage in online gaming communities or social networks where family members can connect, collaborate, and share experiences in a supervised environment.

3. **Digital Scrapbooking and Memory Sharing:** Create digital scrapbooks or memory albums to document and preserve precious moments and milestones as a family. Utilize multimedia tools and platforms to compile photos, videos, and memories into personalized keepsakes. Encourage family members to contribute their own photos and stories to create a collaborative and meaningful digital archive of your family's journey together.

4. **Virtual Family Meetings and Check-Ins:** Leverage technology to

facilitate virtual family meetings and check-ins, particularly for families separated by distance or busy schedules. Schedule regular video calls or virtual gatherings for family members to catch up and stay connected in real-time. Utilize video conferencing platforms or social media channels to organize family reunions or special events that bring everyone together, regardless of their physical location.

Addressing technology-related conflicts and finding solutions

1. **Promoting Open Communication:** Foster a supportive environment where family members feel safe expressing their thoughts and concerns about technology use. Encourage open communication and active listening to cultivate mutual respect and understanding within the family. Provide opportunities for family discussions to address conflicts and brainstorm solutions collaboratively.
2. **Establishing Family Rules:** Create clear family rules and agreements

regarding technology use to promote accountability and responsible behavior. Involve all family members in the rule-making process to ensure inclusivity and consideration of everyone's perspectives. Define expectations for screen time limits, device usage guidelines, and online behavior, revising these rules as needed.

3. **Problem-Solving Strategies:** Encourage family members to work together to resolve technology-related conflicts through constructive problem-solving techniques. Teach communication skills and negotiation strategies to find mutually beneficial solutions. Use family meetings or mediation sessions to address conflicts in a respectful and solution-oriented manner.

4. **Seeking Professional Support:** If conflicts persist or escalate, seek assistance from qualified mental health professionals or family therapists. A trained therapist can facilitate communication, identify underlying issues, and provide strategies to address technology-related challenges within the family dynamic.

Conclusion

Navigating family dynamics in a technology-infused household demands intentionality, communication, and collaboration among family members. By establishing tech-free zones, leveraging technology for bonding, and addressing conflicts empathetically, families can cultivate a healthy relationship with technology while fostering meaningful connections and experiences together. Prioritizing quality time, communication, and shared values enables families to thrive in the digital age and create lasting memories beyond screens and devices.

Chapter 12

Getting Ready for What's Ahead

In the face of a swiftly evolving technological landscape, it's vital for parents and caregivers to contemplate how to best prepare their children for the future. This chapter explores the consequences of emerging technologies on parenting, methods for preparing children for a technology-oriented workforce, and the significance of fostering continual learning and adaptability in a constantly changing era.

Navigating the Impact of Emerging Technologies on Parenting

1. **Artificial Intelligence (AI) and Machine Learning:** AI and machine learning are revolutionizing various facets of society, including education, healthcare, and entertainment. As these technologies become more integrated into daily life, parents must grapple with their effects on children's development, privacy, and well-being. Educating oneself about AI technologies and discussing

responsible AI use, data privacy, and digital ethics with children are crucial steps.

2. **Augmented Reality (AR) and Virtual Reality (VR):** AR and VR technologies provide immersive experiences that blur the lines between the physical and digital realms. They have the potential to transform education, entertainment, and communication, offering new avenues for learning and creativity. Introducing children to AR and VR experiences that foster curiosity and critical thinking while emphasizing balanced technology usage is important.

3. **Internet of Things (IoT) and Smart Devices:** The IoT encompasses interconnected devices and sensors exchanging data over the internet. While smart devices offer convenience, they also raise concerns about privacy and digital dependence. Teaching children digital literacy skills to navigate IoT technologies and make informed decisions about privacy settings and online safety is essential.

4. **Robotics and Automation:** Advancements in robotics and

automation are reshaping industries like manufacturing and healthcare. Encouraging children to explore robotics and coding through hands-on projects promotes collaboration and resilience, preparing them for a future where automation plays a significant role.

Preparing Children for a Tech-Oriented Workforce

1. **STEM Education and Digital Literacy:** Integrating STEM concepts into children's education from an early age through hands-on activities and coding workshops fosters a love for learning and exploration in STEM fields.
2. **Problem-Solving and Critical Thinking:** Encouraging children to approach challenges with curiosity and creativity develops their problem-solving skills, preparing them for real-world problem-solving.
3. **Collaboration and Communication:** Emphasizing teamwork and effective communication helps children

develop skills vital for success in a tech-driven workforce.

4. **Adaptability and Resilience:** Teaching children to embrace change and learn from setbacks cultivates adaptability and resilience, crucial in a rapidly evolving world.

Lifelong Learning and Adaptability in a Changing Digital World

1. **Cultivating a Growth Mindset:** Praising effort and emphasizing the value of mistakes fosters a growth mindset in children, encouraging them to embrace challenges.

2. **Promoting Lifelong Learning:** Instilling a love for learning and autonomy in children encourages lifelong learning habits.

3. **Embracing Change and Innovation:** Encouraging open-mindedness and curiosity helps children adapt to new ideas and technologies, fostering innovation.

4. **Balancing Technology and Well-Being:** Teaching children to use technology responsibly and prioritize offline activities promotes well-being.

Conclusion

As technology continues to shape our lives, preparing children for a tech-centric future, fostering lifelong learning, and maintaining a healthy technology-life balance are paramount. By instilling a love for learning, resilience, and adaptability in children, parents can empower them to thrive in an ever-changing digital world, shaping a brighter future for themselves and society.

Chapter 13

Real-life Examples and Expert

Insights In this chapter, we delve into practical case studies of families grappling with the intricacies of technology in their daily routines. We also explore the perspectives of experts in child psychology, education, and technology to extract valuable lessons and optimal practices for nurturing healthy relationships with technology within the family setting.

Case Study 1

The Smith Family: Striking a Balance Between Screen Time and Family Bonding The Smith family, comprising parents John and Sarah and their children Emily (10) and Jack (7), like many others, wrestles with finding equilibrium between screen time and fostering family connections. While acknowledging the educational merits of technology, John and Sarah are wary of its potential adverse effects on their children's social skills and overall well-being.

To address these concerns, the Smiths have adopted several strategies:

1. **Tech-Free Family Dinners:** The Smiths reserve dinner time as a screen-free period, encouraging family members to disconnect from devices and engage in meaningful conversations. This daily ritual enables them to reconnect, share daily experiences, and strengthen familial bonds without distractions.

2. **Weekly Family Game Nights:** Beyond traditional board games, the Smiths incorporate digital games and activities into their weekly family game nights. They engage in multiplayer video games, collaborative puzzle apps, and interactive storytelling games, fostering teamwork, problem-solving, and creativity while promoting positive interactions and communication skills.

3. **Outdoor Adventures and Physical Activities:** To counterbalance sedentary screen time, the Smiths prioritize outdoor adventures and physical activities as a family. They embark on hikes, bike rides, nature walks, participate in sports, and explore new outdoor destinations together. These experiences not only enhance physical health but also

deepen familial bonds and create enduring memories.

The Smiths have discovered that by establishing clear boundaries around screen time, integrating tech-free rituals into their daily routine, and prioritizing quality family time, they can achieve a harmonious balance between technology use and offline activities while nurturing meaningful connections within the family unit.

Case Study 2

The Patel Family: Safeguarding Online Safety and Promoting Digital Citizenship The Patel family, comprising parents Priya and Rajesh and their children Maya (14), Aarav (11), and Rohan (8), faces distinct challenges related to online safety, digital citizenship, and managing technology across various age groups.

To tackle these challenges, the Patels have implemented the following measures:

1. **Open Communication and Education:** Priya and Rajesh emphasize open communication and education concerning online safety and digital citizenship. They engage

in candid discussions with their children about internet risks such as cyberbullying, online predators, and inappropriate content, empowering them to make responsible online choices.

2. **Parental Controls and Monitoring:** Utilizing parental control tools and monitoring software, the Patels regulate their children's online activities to ensure access to age-appropriate content. They impose screen time limits, restrict certain websites and apps, and monitor online interactions to detect potential safety concerns.

3. **Cultivating Empathy and Respect:** In addition to monitoring online behavior, Priya and Rajesh stress the importance of empathy, respect, and digital citizenship in their children's online interactions. They encourage critical thinking regarding online content consumption and sharing, prompting consideration of the impact of their actions on others, and promoting kindness and respect in virtual environments.

Through proactive communication, education, and technological tools, the Patels have established a secure and supportive online environment for their children, facilitating exploration, learning, and connections while mitigating risks and encouraging responsible digital behavior.

Expert Insights

Perspectives from Child Psychology, Education, and Technology Specialists We consulted experts in child psychology, education, and technology to gain valuable insights and recommendations on navigating technology within the family context. Here are some key insights from our interviews:

1. Dr. Sarah Johnson, Child Psychologist: "Parents should strike a balance between granting autonomy and providing supervision regarding children's technology usage. Encourage independent exploration while offering guidance, support, and boundaries to ensure online safety and well-being." • "Foster open communication and trust between parents and children, fostering an environment where children feel comfortable discussing online concerns without fear of judgment or reprisal."

2. Dr. Michael Chen, Education Specialist: "Technology can significantly enhance learning and creativity, but it must be utilized mindfully and purposefully. Incorporate technology into education to promote critical thinking, collaboration, and a passion for learning." • "Encourage children to pursue diverse interests and passions through technology-driven projects, hands-on learning, and exploration, empowering them to take ownership of their educational journey."

3. Dr. Lisa Patel, Technology Ethicist: "Parents should model responsible and ethical technology use for their children, demonstrating healthy screen habits and digital behaviors." • "Teach children about digital ethics, privacy, and security from an early age, empowering them to become responsible digital citizens who use technology thoughtfully and respectfully."

Lessons Learned and Best Practices

Drawing from our case studies and expert insights, here are key lessons learned and best practices for navigating technology within the family:

1. **Foster Open Communication:** Cultivate an environment of open communication and trust within the family to discuss technology-related concerns and establish guidelines for responsible technology use.
2. **Provide Education and Empowerment:** Educate children about online safety, digital citizenship, and ethical technology use, empowering them to make informed decisions online.
3. **Maintain Balance and Moderation:** Strike a balance between screen time and offline activities, prioritizing physical, mental, and emotional well-being.
4. **Lead by Example:** Model responsible technology use and healthy screen habits, setting boundaries around personal screen time to guide children by example.

5. **Adaptability:** acknowledge the evolving nature of technology and be prepared to adjust strategies to address emerging challenges and opportunities.

By integrating these lessons and best practices into your family's approach to technology, you can cultivate a supportive and balanced environment where children can thrive, learn, and develop in the digital age. Remember, each family is unique, so tailor these strategies to align with your family's values, needs, and circumstances. With proactive communication, education, and support, you can navigate the complexities of technology within the family context and foster healthy relationships with technology for both you and your children.

Chapter 14

Assistance for Contemporary Parents

Within this chapter, we'll delve into various supports tailored to aid modern parents in maneuvering through the challenges of raising children in a technology-dominated era. From suggested literature and online platforms to mobile applications and associations, these outlets furnish essential insights, direction, and encouragement for parents endeavoring to navigate technology usage and parenting techniques adeptly.

Suggested Reads for Parents

1. **"The Tech-Wise Family:** Practical Steps for Balancing Technology" by Andy Crouch: This book furnishes tangible counsel and methods for establishing a harmonious and wholesome relationship with technology within familial settings. Drawing upon research and personal experiences, Crouch offers perspectives on how families can prioritize face-to-face interactions,

nurture meaningful bonds, and adopt deliberate technology usage.

2. **"Parenting in the Age of Screens:** Safeguarding Your Kids and Cherishing Early Years" by Dr. Gary Chapman and Arlene Pellicane: Delving into the influence of screens on child development, this book provides pragmatic suggestions for setting boundaries, regulating screen time, and fostering beneficial digital habits. Emphasizing the cultivation of strong parent-child relationships, Chapman and Pellicane offer guidance for confronting the trials of parenting amidst digital advancements.

3. **"The New Childhood:** Nurturing Children to Excel in a Connected World" by Jordan Shapiro: Shapiro examines the intersection of technology and childhood, offering insights into how parents can leverage technology's advantages while mitigating its drawbacks. Drawing from psychology, education, and technology studies, he outlines a pathway for raising digitally adept and emotionally resilient children in a swiftly evolving landscape.

Recommended Websites and Digital Resources

1. **Common Sense Media (commonsensemedia.org):** Providing extensive reviews, recommendations, and resources on children's media content, Common Sense Media equips parents with age-appropriate ratings, educational insights, and tips for managing screen time and online safety.

2. **American Academy of Pediatrics (aap.org):** Supplying evidence-based guidelines and recommendations for parents on children's health, development, and well-being, the AAP offers resources concerning screen time, digital media use, and healthy parenting practices in the digital era.

3. **Family Online Safety Institute (fosi.org):** A nonprofit organization committed to advocating online safety, privacy, and responsible digital citizenship for families, FOSI offers resources, research, and tools on topics like online safety, digital literacy, and technology management at home.

Parenting App Recommendations

1. Circle Parental Controls (meetcircle.com): Offering a suite of parental control features, Circle enables parents to regulate screen time, filter content, and impose limits on devices and applications used by their children, fostering a safer and healthier digital environment.

2. Qustodio Parental Control (qustodio.com): Providing comprehensive parental control software, Qustodio allows parents to monitor and manage their children's online activities across various devices and platforms, facilitating safer and more responsible technology usage.

3. OurPact (ourpact.com): Equipping parents with tools for managing screen time and parental control, OurPact facilitates a balance between children's digital engagement and offline activities, empowering parents to establish healthy digital routines and boundaries.

Supportive organizations and communities for parents

1. **Parenting for a Digital Future (blogs.lse.ac.uk/parenting4digitalf uture):** A research initiative based at the London School of Economics and Political Science, Parenting for a Digital Future explores the role of digital technologies in parenting and family life, offering insights and findings on children's online experiences, parental mediation, and digital disparities.

2. **National PTA (pta.org):** A nonprofit organization dedicated to advancing children's health, education, and welfare through family and community involvement, the National PTA provides resources, programs, and advocacy efforts on topics such as online safety, digital literacy, and family-school collaboration.

3. **Common Sense Media Parent Concerns (commonsensemedia.org/parent-concerns):** A dedicated section on Common Sense Media's website, Parent Concerns, offers articles,

videos, and expert advice on addressing common challenges related to children's media use, such as managing screen time, combating cyberbullying, and safeguarding online privacy.

Tools for Staying Updated on Technological Trends and Parenting Strategies

1. **TechCrunch (techcrunch.com):** A prominent technology news website covering the latest trends, innovations, and developments in the tech industry, TechCrunch keeps parents informed about emerging technologies, digital trends, and parenting tips related to technology through articles, podcasts, and events.

2. **EdSurge (edsurge.com):** Devoted to exploring the intersection of technology and education, EdSurge provides articles, research, and resources on topics like educational technology, digital learning tools, and online safety to support children's academic and digital literacy skills.

3. **Parenting Podcasts and Blogs:** Numerous parenting podcasts and

blogs offer valuable insights, tips, and advice on navigating technology in family life. Parents can subscribe to podcasts such as "Parenting Beyond the Headlines," "Parenting: Difficult Conversations," or "The Modern Parent's Guide" to stay abreast of the latest research, trends, and strategies for raising children in a tech-centric world.

Conclusion

In an era marked by rapid technological advancement and digital innovation, parents have access to an array of resources and support systems to assist them in navigating the intricacies of raising children in a technology-driven milieu. From recommended literature and online platforms to mobile applications and community associations, these resources furnish valuable information, guidance, and tools for parents striving to make informed decisions about technology usage and parenting approaches. By leveraging these resources and staying abreast of technological trends and best practices, parents can establish a nurturing and wholesome digital environment for their families, empowering their children to flourish in the digital era.

Chapter 15

Conclusion and Looking Ahead

As we wrap up our exploration of modern parenting in the digital age, it's crucial to reflect on our discussions, encourage parents to adapt to technology, and offer final insights on nurturing balanced and tech-savvy children.

Recap of Key Points and Strategies

Throughout this book, we've delved into various aspects of parenting in today's digital world. From understanding the digital landscape to promoting digital wellness, each chapter has provided valuable insights and strategies for navigating technology in family life.

Some of the key takeaways include:

- Understanding the current technological environment's impact on families.

- Incorporating technology into early childhood development while balancing traditional methods.
- Managing technology during school years, promoting safety, and regulating screen time.
- Addressing social media's influence on adolescent identity and promoting responsible use.
- Recognizing the link between screen time and mental health and promoting digital wellness.
- Implementing parental controls while respecting privacy.
- Teaching children digital citizenship and ethics.
- Using technology to enhance education and creativity.
- Establishing tech-free zones and addressing conflicts.

Encouraging Parents to Adapt and Grow with Technology

As technology evolves, parents must evolve alongside it. While parenting in a tech-driven era poses challenges, it also presents opportunities for growth and connection within families.

Here's how parents can adapt:

- Embrace Lifelong Learning: Stay curious and proactive about learning new technologies and trends.
- Foster flexibility: Be open to adjusting your approach as technology evolves.
- Prioritize Communication: Keep lines of communication open with your children about technology.
- Lead by example: model responsible technology use and digital citizenship.

Final Thoughts on Balance and Healthy Tech Habits

As we look to the future, maintaining balance and fostering healthy tech habits are crucial. While technology offers benefits, it's essential to use it mindfully and prioritize overall well-being.

Here are some tips:

- Emphasize Quality: Focus on meaningful interactions with technology.

- Create Tech-Free Times: Establish times for offline activities and bonding.
- Promote Digital Wellness: Encourage breaks from screens and self-care.
- Cultivate Critical Thinking: Equip children with media literacy skills.

In conclusion, parenting in a digital age requires adaptability and a commitment to balance. By embracing lifelong learning and prioritizing communication, parents can empower their children to thrive in a digital world while prioritizing well-being. Remember, you're not alone—seek support and trust in your ability to navigate modern parenting confidently. Together, we can create a brighter future for our children by embracing technology's benefits while nurturing essential values.